PRAYER OF THE HEART

An Approach to Silent Prayer

and

PRAYER IN THE NIGHT

Alexander Ryrie

SLG Press
Convent of the Incarnation
Fairacres Oxford

ISBN 0 7283 0140 X
ISSN 0307-1405

Printed by Will Print, Oxford

ACKNOWLEDGEMENTS

We are grateful to the following for permission to quote from
published works: Faber and Faber Ltd., *The Art of Prayer*, edited by
Timothy Ware, 1966; HarperCollins, *Be Still and Know* by Michael
Ramsey, 1982; Oxford University Press, *Michael Ramsey, A Life* by
Owen Chadwick, 1990. Bible quotations are from the NRSV

PRAYER OF THE HEART

WHERE do you begin if you want to engage in silent prayer? What are the first steps? There are, of course, different approaches, and no single one of them will suit everybody. Here I will try very simply to outline one way which has been of help to a number of people. To do this I want to use a sentence from one of the greatest Russian spiritual writers, St Theophan the Recluse. He said:

> The principal thing is to stand with the mind in the heart before God, and to go on standing before him unceasingly day and night until the end of life *(The Art of Prayer, p.63).*

Silent prayer is the 'prayer of the heart'. We engage in it by 'descending into the heart', and 'standing before God with the mind in the heart'. What does this mean?

Heart and Mind

We will start by thinking what we mean by the 'heart' and the 'mind', most importantly the 'heart'. Our heart in this context does not mean our feelings. It means our inner self, our inmost self. The true, the real 'Me'; the inner Me that is tucked away deep down within us, which we do not reveal or show to anyone else, perhaps not even to ourselves. We may perhaps feel or sense it as the original Me—the Me that was originally there in our earliest childhood, when we can first remember being conscious of ourselves. There is an inmost self that gets hidden, covered over by all sorts of things, but it is there in all of us, underneath everything. This is the heart.

It is not just an idea. The heart is a real part of us, and we locate it in our bodies. We are not, of course, talking about our physical heart, the body's pump; but we are aware that so long as we live in this physical life we find our true, inmost self within our physical bodies. We don't find our heart by escaping from our bodies into something 'spiritual'. We find it by putting ourselves within ourselves, within our bodies.

The reason we go down into our heart is that it is the place where we meet God, or rather, where God meets us. That is not to say that God is the same as our heart; or that by finding our heart or going down into it we automatically find God. Nor is it to say that this is the only place where God is to be found. God, the infinite creator of all that is, cannot be confined within the universe, let alone in one small heart. Nevertheless, he meets us in our hearts. And we go down into the heart not because it feels nice, or even because it does us good, but because that is where we encounter God, where we 'stand before God'.

So the heart is the place of prayer. Prayer is essentially not something which we do with our minds nor with our words, no matter how much we may use both our minds and our words in prayer. Prayer is something which we do in our hearts.

But of course it is not quite as simple as that. For most of us, our hearts are not all that easily accessible. There are two reasons for this. The first is that our hearts have got overlaid by all sorts of things. Over the years we have unconsciously developed patterns of self-protecting and self-boosting thoughts and attitudes. We are not sure that our true self will be acceptable to other people. And we are not sure that our inmost self is acceptable to *us*. Being 'Me' is a pretty uncertain, risky, perhaps even frightening, thing. I am the only Me there is. I am not certain that I like being that original, inmost Me. And I am not at all certain that other people will like that Me. So unintentionally and unconsciously we develop ways of covering up that Me. Without realising it we put on a kind of act much of the time. We pretend we are like other people. We try to make ourselves into what we would like to be, or what we think other people expect us to be, or what we feel we ought to be. And the real Me—the heart—gets covered up by layers of this kind of thing which develop over the years. To reach the heart we need to get below these layers.

In passing I must say that this is not the same thing as either facing or dealing with what is in these layers. There may be painful, difficult things within ourselves, and sometimes it is important to face and deal with them. However, to go down into the heart we do not need to deal with all the troublesome things within us: we need to go below them.

The second thing that makes our heart inaccessible is simply the ordinary thoughts and feelings which keep crowding in upon us. Our minds are full of all sorts of things, and they probably jump from one thing to another, even when, perhaps especially when, we are trying to pray. All of that goes on in our heads, and we need to get away from it if we are really going to pray. As St Theophan also says: 'The head is a crowded rag-market: it is not possible to pray to God there' (p. 184). We have got to focus our attention not on all the things that are crowding into our heads, but on our hearts. When we talk of 'the mind in the heart', that is what we mean. The 'mind' means the attention. We have to focus our attention on our hearts, because the heart is a still place. When we go down into it we are still; we get away from the crowded rag-market of our heads. It is in that stillness that we stand before God, and are open to God.

Putting the Mind Into the Heart

How then do we put the mind into the heart? The first requirement is *stillness*. Stillness is not just silence in the sense of freedom from noise or speech. Of course this kind of silence is necessary. We need to stop talking and to be in a situation where we are not distracted by other sounds. We can do this either by putting ourselves in a very quiet place, or by learning to shut out other sounds from our minds and attention. But stillness is more than that. It has three levels.

First, there is *stillness of body*. We need to get into a bodily posture in which we are sufficiently relaxed, but also attentive. No part of our body must be drawing special attention to itself. Secondly, there is *stillness of mind*. This is much harder to achieve. We must allow the chatter of our thoughts and feelings to die down. We will consider shortly some ways in which this can be done. Thirdly, there is *stillness of spirit*. We only reach this when our bodies and minds are still. Our spirit is that aspect of us which relates to God. To engage in silent prayer we have to reach the point where we are not clambering after God, not asking for anything from God, but just being still before God.

To make ourselves still we need to become aware of what is going on within us, and to be honest about ourselves and our feelings. The first requirement of prayer is honesty. It is amazing how often we fail to recognise what we are really feeling, or what lies behind our feelings. So it is useful to take a few minutes to ask ourselves: What am I really feeling? What is going on in me? Are there things niggling away, or going round and round within me, or giving me a sad feeling or a good feeling? Recognising these things and opening them up to ourselves is important, because they can lie between ourselves and our heart.

Then it is useful to *focus*, and by that I mean focus with our eyes. If we close our eyes and direct them to one spot within ourselves, preferably to our hearts, and try to keep them focused, that helps us to be still.

Rhythm Prayer

The most helpful and useful way to become still and descend into the heart is through a 'rhythm prayer'. This is a very short form of words which make up a prayer, and which is repeated quietly over and over again within oneself. It can be any little prayer: 'O God help!'; 'Come Lord'; 'Lord, here I am'; 'O God make speed to save me'; or perhaps a slightly longer phrase or sentence. One can adopt any form of rhythm prayer one chooses. In the Orthodox Church there is a long tradition of using the Jesus Prayer: 'Lord Jesus Christ, Son of God, have mercy upon me'—or some variant of that. In fact, there is a whole spiritual approach, almost a way of life, based on the use of the Jesus Prayer. But whatever form of words we use, the rhythm prayer is repeated quietly over and over again along with our breathing—saying it as we breathe in and again as we breathe out; or the first part as we breathe in and the second as we breathe out.

There are two things to be noted about using a rhythm prayer. The first is that a rhythm prayer is not a 'mantra'—a special formula used in Asiatic religions to help people to enter into themselves. It is a *prayer*. Its purpose is partly to remind us that we are engaged in approaching God and standing before him, and partly to invite God to come and help us.

The second thing to note is that a rhythm prayer is a means by which our attention becomes focused. We need to put our mind, our attention, into the heart. We need to make our minds still. But our attention keeps flying all over the place, constantly distracted, usually flitting from one thing to another. So we concentrate our attention on the words of the rhythm prayer as we repeat it over and over again. If, as usually happens in spite of this, we find ourselves distracted, we return to the words of the rhythm prayer. It is not a magic formula; it is not a way of conjuring up God; but it is to help us to focus our attention, to come out of the 'crowded rag-market' of our heads into our hearts.

It is useful to set aside a certain time when we do nothing else but remain still and repeat our rhythm prayer over and over again before God. In this way we get more deeply into it; it becomes more natural, and we find ourselves becoming still and getting down into the heart more easily. But it does not need to be limited to one special time of day. We can say it at any time quietly within ourselves. Every now and then we pause and say as we breathe in and out: 'O God help me', 'Come Lord Jesus', 'Lord Jesus Christ, Son of God, have mercy upon me', or whatever our rhythm prayer is. In fact, if we go on saying the phrase often enough, we begin to find it coming naturally. We find it coming back again and again during the day, or as we lie awake at night. And it can

become what St Theophan calls a 'murmuring stream'—
something that is going on within us all the time. That is a
long way off for most of us; but any of us can begin to use a
rhythm prayer to help us descend into the heart.

However, for most of us even the rhythm prayer doesn't
give *immediate* access to the heart. There is so much else going
on within us, so much chatter that must die down, so many
layers inside us, that it takes a while to reach stillness and get
into the heart. Archbishop Michael Ramsey, who was a
committed user of the Jesus Prayer, wrote in *Be Still and
Know:* 'The repetition, many times and many times, is found
to quieten the distracting parts of our personalities, and to
keep us wonderfully subdued and concentrated.' But also, as
Owen Chadwick relates in his biography, *Michael Ramsey, A
Life,* he was once asked by an American reporter whether he
had prayed that day, and for how long he had talked to God.
He replied: 'I talked to God for one minute. But it took me
twenty-nine minutes to get there.'

The Presence of God

This kind of prayer is not praying *for* anything. It is not even
talking to God, at any rate not all the time. It is not a matter of
asking for things for ourselves, or even for other people. All
that has a place in prayer, but not in *this* kind of prayer. Silent
prayer, the prayer of the heart, is simply a matter of being still
before God for his sake, and nothing else. Because God is God
—God of greatness, glory, majesty, graciousness and love—
we want simply to *be* with him, to stand before him.

We can take steps to descend into the heart and make
ourselves still before God; but what happens next is up to
God, not to us. Standing before God means waiting. We wait
for the Lord. The heart is the place where God is present; but
we don't command or control God's presence, or the sense of
his presence. We cannot expect that whenever and as soon as
we choose to descend into the heart, God will automatically
and immediately be there, making his presence felt. God is
God; he is a free agent. He is not to be conjured up or

manipulated, so that we can make him present or ignore him when we want. If we want to be in the presence of God and to know his presence, we have to wait: to wait upon the Lord, to tarry for his good pleasure, to be ready to meet him when he comes to us, to acknowledge his presence when he reveals it to us; and for the rest of the time simply to wait. To use the language of the Old Testament, God shows his face and he hides his face.

And what happens when God makes himself present? It is different for different people. Some people have a very vivid sense of God which comes to them easily and frequently. They are given a rich experience of his presence. Some experience only a vague *something*—perhaps something they are aware of *after* their time of silence rather than during it. Some people really experience nothing at all; but they come to know that as they continue in silence day by day somehow God is present.

Often we may go through times when the whole thing seems pointless; but we discover that it is still worth doing, because we are putting ourselves into the hand of God, focusing on him and waiting for him, and that is enough. It is not about our feelings; we do not do it to have feelings or experiences. We do it for God, and for God alone. We put ourselves before him and leave it at that, whether we have feelings or not.

In fact, the whole business of feelings and experiences can be very misleading. The spiritual fathers of old used to warn people against experiences. If we have experiences or special feelings as we stand before God, these may be illusions or delusions, things which arise from our own psyche, our own mind and emotions, because we want them to happen. They may have nothing to do with God, so we have to distrust them. If they are from God they will lead us more towards God: they will help us to focus on him, draw us towards him and make us love him. If they are from ourselves they will make us think of ourselves and of what we are experiencing; then they need to be gently set aside.

So as we stand before God with the mind in the heart there may be nothing happening that we are conscious of. But in fact something does happen. There is a deep converse with God: a meeting with God at depth that we may not even be aware of; an engagement between ourselves and God in the deep, hidden and largely unconscious recesses of ourselves, which is initiated by God himself, and not by us. It is that deep converse of God with our hearts that constitutes the prayer of the heart. It is not something that we can do. It is something that God does within us. We can prepare for it; we can descend into the heart and wait for it. But we cannot bring it about, and we may not even know that it is happening. It is what is sometimes called 'pure prayer'— prayer which comes from God to us, rather than from us to God.

There are people who become drawn deeply into this kind of prayer, who give much of their lives to waiting upon God in this way, and for whom this kind of pure prayer is a constant reality. But even if not many of us are in that category, most of us can take the first simple steps; the rest is up to God.

Confession and Intercession

From what has been said so far it may seem as if this kind of praying is an isolated thing, a thing which we do all by itself. But how is the prayer of the heart related to the rest of our life and the rest of our praying?

We saw earlier that when we descend into the heart we go down through what I have called the layers of our inner life. In the first layer are all the relatively superficial things, the thoughts and feelings which are going on in us, the things we are worrying about, the things our minds are concerned with. Below these are the layers of deeper, more hidden things: our secret fears and guilty feelings; our deep anxieties about ourselves, the ways we have developed of protecting ourselves, of boosting ourselves, of pretending to be something; layers which we are aware of, and layers which we are not aware of or feel unable to face or enter.

As we make a habit of descending into the heart we become conscious that we are going down through all these layers which make up an inner world, some of which are unknown even to ourselves. As we enter our heart, we bring this inner world down into the heart, not in the sense that we continue to be preoccupied with it, but so that we can place it before God. We lay it down before God and let it go. We lay down before God all the thoughts and feelings and all the deeper things that are within us, and leave them there.

This then becomes one form, the deepest form, of the prayer of confession. I said earlier that the first step towards descending into the heart is honesty, trying to be aware of what is going on in us. We become more aware of what we are really like: how mixed up we are inside, how mixed our motives are, how much pretending goes on. We may also realise that there are things we feel guilty about. Going down into the heart does not mean avoiding these things, but rather taking them down with us and laying them before God as we stand before him in silence. This is our prayer of confession.

It is similar with our intercessions. There will be within us concerns and worries and thoughts about other people and situations: people who are on our minds because we love them, or are worried about them, or because they have hurt us and we hate them and cannot get on with them, or simply because we have been meeting them. There may be situations and circumstances that are bothering us. When we descend into the heart we do not just give up or ignore these people and things as irrelevant. We take them down into the heart and lay them before God, leaving them before God and entrusting them to him. We do not go on thinking and worrying about them, nor try to persuade God to do something about them, but just leave them before him, waiting on him, allowing him to act.

Standing before God with the mind in the heart thus becomes the deepest form of both our confession and our intercession. There are, of course, other forms of intercession and prayer. There are the more conscious forms, the spoken prayers, the talking with God, the petitions and requests. These go on as well. But if our standing before God in the silence of our heart has any reality, then it underlies all our other praying. Our other prayers, our articulated intercessions, are prayers to the God before whom we have stood with the mind in the heart. If we continue to use a rhythm prayer as often as possible, we begin to discover that we stand before God all the time. So our habit of standing before God becomes the basis of all our other praying, and lends depth and reality to it.

But the prayer of the heart is intercession in yet another sense. When we stand before God, we open ourselves to him and so make a way for him to come and work within us. But we do this not as isolated individuals; we are part of a larger world. In putting ourselves at God's disposal we are making a way for God to come to one little bit of his world. If we want him to come to his world, which is what our intercessions are about, if we want his kingdom to come as we pray, the first thing to do, and perhaps the most important thing to do, is to lay ourselves before God, and wait for him to start with us, deep within our own hearts. In other words, there is a sense in which, by standing before God, we do not *say* prayers of intercession, but we, in some measure at least, *become* intercession. We become a prayer, a small means by which God comes into his world.

Sr Benedicta has said of the Desert Fathers, who gave their whole lives to silence and prayer and standing before God, that in their doing this, 'one part of torn and broken humanity [was] placed before its Saviour' (*Lives of the Desert Fathers*, p.13). When any of us engages in the prayer of the heart, one part of the torn and broken humanity of which we are all part is laid before God. And there is nothing more profound or important that we can do for the needs of the world than that.

PRAYER IN THE NIGHT

Let every prayer you offer in the night be more precious
in your eyes than all your activities of the day.

THESE words written in the seventh century by Isaac of Nineveh[1] remind us that prayer in the night has had an important part in Christian spirituality throughout the centuries. The tradition goes back, of course, beyond Christian times to the Old Testament, where psalmists speak of praying, meditating, and calling on God during the hours of the night:

> When I think of you on my bed,
> and meditate on you in the watches of the night.
>
> (Ps. 63:6)
>
> I commune with my heart in the night;
> I meditate and search my spirit.
>
> (Ps. 77:6)
>
> When at night, I cry out in your presence,
> let my prayer come before you.
>
> (Ps. 88:1-2)

Elsewhere in the Old Testament, the prophet Isaiah speaks of longing for God during the night:

> My soul yearns for you in the night,
> my spirit within me earnestly seeks you.
>
> (Isa. 26:9)

Other verses suggest that some devout people got up during the night to praise God:

> At midnight I rise to praise you,
> because of your righteous judgements.
>
> (Ps. 119:62)

and that others kept vigil in the temple throughout the night:

> Come, bless the Lord, all you servants of the Lord,
> who stand by night in the house of the Lord!
>
> (Ps. 134:1)

11

When we come to the New Testament, the Gospels testify to Jesus' practice of going off by himself to spend the night or the very early hours of the morning in prayer. 'In those days', says Luke, 'he went out into the hills to pray, and all night he continued in prayer to God' (Luke 5:12; see also Mark 1:35; Matt. 14:23-25).

It is not surprising, therefore, that the practice of night prayer was continued by the early Christians, especially by the monks, ascetics and solitaries. The Desert Fathers attached a great deal of importance to night vigils, many of them spending the whole night in prayer and psalmody,[2] and this tradition continued amongst the monks and ascetics of the east. Isaac of Nineveh, who was one of the most influential of the spiritual writers of the east, put special emphasis on night prayer and vigil, and discussed it at some length. 'Do not imagine', he said, 'that among all the works of monastics there is any practice greater than night vigil.' Prayer during the night, he maintained, yielded a very special joy. It was 'a work filled with delight', and those who engaged in it could experience 'an onrush of joy that surges in their souls.'[3]

Isaac wrote mainly with solitaries in mind, and thought of night prayer largely as an individual activity, but he emphasised that for monks it should include an office, and follow a certain rule, including prayers, psalms, hymns and readings. Under the Rule of St Benedict it was developed into a formal Night Office for monks living in community. Indeed, the Rule gives more attention to the form and practice of the Night Office than to any of the other offices, laying down the precise hour of 2 a.m., specifying some of the psalms to be sung, and making different arrangements for summer and winter. From then until our own day, the Night Office has continued in the western monastic tradition, as it has in the east.

But alongside this monastic tradition there is another strand. We have evidence from early days that prayer in the night was undertaken not only by monks and solitaries, but also by lay people in their own homes. The third century author of the *Apostolic Tradition* encouraged Christians in

Rome to pray in the night. 'Towards the middle of the night', he writes, 'get up, wash your hands in water, and pray.'[4] And in Constantinople in the fourth century John Chrysostom called on his people to attend night services and devotions, because 'when darkness and silence enfold everything, our minds are purer, lighter, and more spiritually alert'.[5] There is, of course, no way of knowing to what extent this practice has been maintained by individual Christian people over the years, but there is good reason to believe that a considerable number of ordinary people still find themselves drawn to prayer in one way or another during the night. This is a strand of prayer which inevitably and rightly remains largely hidden and secret, an underground stream of devotion which is silent and unseen, but it is nevertheless an important element in the church's offering to God.

Why Prayer in the Night?

'Prayer offered up at night', says Isaac, 'possesses great power, greater than the prayer of the daytime.' Why should this be? What is special about the night, that people should use it in a particular way for prayer? Perhaps the basic point here is that the night is a time of emptiness or nothingness between two days. Prayer in the night is undertaken most especially in the 'dead of night', the time of 'no-day' between yesterday and tomorrow, when things of yesterday have come to an end and the things of tomorrow have not yet begun. It is, therefore, a time when it is more easy to stand aside from the things of yesterday and tomorrow, and turn to God himself. The English mystic, Walter Hilton, writing of the desire for God in the night, says: 'You know well that a night is a space between two days, for when one day is ended another comes: not at once, but night comes first to divide the days.' So for him the physical night stands for a deep spiritual night, which is 'nothing but a separation of the soul from earthly things, by great desire and yearning to love, see and feel Jesus and the things of the spirit.'[6] This empty time is usually a time of darkness, silence and solitude, when we see

13

nothing, hear nothing, say nothing, do nothing, and have no direct relation with anyone else. It is a desert time, and in this desert it can be specially easy to draw near to God. It is a time of mystery, of the reality of things unseen, of the closeness of God. A time when we can be aware of what Henry Vaughan calls the 'deep but dazzling darkness' that is in God.

Because of this, the night can be a rich, warm time, filled with the 'delight' and the 'onrush of joy' of which Isaac speaks. Vaughan expresses this in his poem *The Night,*[7] inspired by the Nicodemus incident in John 3:

> Dear Night! this world's defeat;
> The stop to busy fools; care's check and curb;
> The day of Spirits; my soul's calm retreat
>   Which none disturb!
> Christ's progress, and his prayer time;
> The hours to which high heaven doth chime.
>
> Were all my loud, evil days
> Calm and unhaunted as is thy dark tent,
> Whose peace but by some Angels wing or voice
>   Is seldom rent;
> Then I in Heaven all the long year
> Would keep, and never wander here.

And he concludes by expressing his longing for the night:

> O for that night! where I in him
> Might live invisible and dim.

But the night is not always a time of joy. In the hours of darkness, at the dead of night feelings of a very different kind, of anxiety, loneliness, depression or fear, can rise up to haunt and torment us. And for some it is a time when pain becomes particularly hard to bear. This too can add a special quality to the prayer of the night, making it not a matter of delight, but an occasion of crying out to God for comfort and relief. And perhaps it becomes a time when we discover that God is ultimately our only comforter.

For some the night can also have a further quality. It can be a time when evil seems to be a particularly powerful reality, when the powers of darkness are especially active, and the 'perils and dangers of the night' are at hand. The fathers and mothers of the desert thought of evil in the form of demons, and their hours of vigil during the night were in a special way times of struggle against them. Night prayer was a time of keeping watch, of guarding the heart against evil. It was a following of the injunction of Jesus to 'watch and pray lest you enter into temptation'.

Elements of Night Prayer

If these are some of the special characteristics of the night season, what will be the nature and content of prayer in the night? The character and quality of individual prayer, as opposed to the office of a monastic community will, of course, vary a great deal from one person to another. There is no one single pattern, but perhaps it is possible to identify some basic elements which can be included in it.

One element is very simple and basic: it is the opening of oneself to the special sense of the mystery of God which is one of the gifts offered by the darkness and stillness of the night. Taking a little time to be aware of this mystery, and to be still before the deep but dazzling darkness of God, can be an important element in the prayer of the night.

Another appropriate element is praise, which can be expressed in different ways, perhaps through the words of psalm, canticle, hymn, or perhaps through the silent adoration of the heart. Praise is the basic substructure of prayer, and the night is a time for praise. The dead of night, the time when everything else stops, can be felt to be very specially a time when all creation is offering its silent chorus of praise, and it is possible, in the silence of the night, to join imaginatively in this offering. The *Apostolic Tradition*, gives this as one of the special reasons for prayer in the dead of night:

> We have to pray at this hour because the men of old from whom we have received this tradition have taught us that all creation rests then for a moment in order to praise the Lord. The stars, the trees, the rivers stop for an instant and, together with the choir of angels and the souls of the righteous, sing the praises of God. And so praying at this hour ought to be precious to the faithful.[8]

Petition and intercession can also take on a special quality in the night. If we ourselves are taken over by pain or anxiety or grief, we may find ourselves able to do no more than to cry out to God in the night for help. As with the psalmist, our petition may have to be, in the first instance at least, for ourselves:

> O Lord, God of my salvation,
>   When, at night, I cry out in your presence,
> let my prayer come before you;
>   incline your ear to my cry.
> For my soul is full of troubles.
>
> (Ps. 88:1-3)

But the season when most people are asleep is also a good time to remember others who are awake. Evagrius, in the fourth century, urged his readers to overcome their own sluggishness by thinking of the many people who have to be up in the night. 'When you want to get up to pray during the night', he says, 'and your body is feeling sluggish, ... recollect how many are awake and at their work, how many are travelling on journeys, are ploughing (*sic*!), or carrying on various crafts; remember the shepherds, the night watchmen, those guarding their treasures.'[9] The thought that others are awake and at work may or may not work as an incentive to us, but it can be a theme for intercession. We can remember with thankfulness those on whose labours during the night we depend for some basic necessities. We can also make a prayer for those who are awake because they cannot sleep as a result of pain, grief, anxiety, fear, or other troubles; and for parts of the world where night brings no peace. And perhaps a special prayer for those who, during the night, are drawing near to death. Along with these we can also remember others, known and unknown, who like us are engaged, secretly and in silence, in the prayer of the night. There is a rich vein of petition of a special kind which can be tapped during the hours of darkness.

Finally, there is the element of vigil. By this I mean not simply keeping awake and silent before God, but being on guard against evil. As I said earlier, there are some who are especially aware of the presence of evil during the night, either as a hostile power, or simply as non-being. Others without this particular awareness can use the silence and mystery of the night to be aware of the 'passions' and the operation of the powers of darkness within their own hearts—the distorted feelings, twisted motives, self-centred longings and desires, and the faithless anxieties which tend to take over our inner selves—and to acknowledge the contribution these make to the world's evils and sufferings which are borne in upon us during the night. This vigil of guarding the heart can be an important element in the prayer of the night.

Different Practices

Some of these elements may be common to the night prayer of many people, but our different sleep patterns and diverse states of feeling and awareness during the night, added to our differences in consciousness of God and in the practice of prayer generally, will mean that people will approach night prayer in very different ways. Some, following the monastic tradition, will observe it as an office, with a structure of psalmody, canticle, *kyries* and the Lord's Prayer. Others will keep it as a time of silent contemplation, or of personal prayers and petitions. It is clear from personal communications that many people who find themselves awake for some time during the night use these times of wakefulness as opportunities for prayer. One writes of lying in bed and quietly reciting the Lord's Prayer, followed by prayers for others. Another comments that many of her intercessions are done while lying awake at night. But others find it helpful to give a more formal structure to their prayer. One rises to observe a half hour, using a formal office, and another repeats a version of the Benedicite, praising God for all creation.

There are also some who, in keeping with what I said earlier, are particularly conscious of evil and the powers of darkness. One describes the experience of being plunged during the darkness into an empty nothingness and sense of non-being, which is only dispelled by 'grateful adoration'. Another writes of 'a close encounter with evil in its intangible and tangible forms', and adds that 'night is a time when it is more likely to happen'.

So the prayer of the night takes many forms and is practised in different ways. Its preservation as a formal Night Office in monasteries and convents has been immensely important and often an encouragement and comfort to others. But the tradition has also been preserved in a more hidden, unorganised and apparently haphazard way by unknown numbers of individual people who have kept vigil in their own privacy and silence, holding themselves quietly before God in the dead of night, in contemplation, in praise, in petition for themselves and others, and in watchfulness against evil; and in this way taking part in a secret, hidden stream of prayer while the world sleeps.

NOTES

[1] Quoted in Hilarion Alfeyev, *The Spiritual World of Isaac the Syrian*, Kalamazoo, Cistercian Publications, 2000, p.184.

[2] See, for example, *The Lives of the Desert Fathers*, London, Mowbray, 1981, p.77; *Sayings of the Desert Fathers*, London, Mowbray, 1975, p.14. Arsenius 30.

[3] H. Alfeyev, *op. cit.*, pp. 184, 190.

[4] Quoted in O. Clément, *The Roots of Christian Mysticism*, London, New City, 1993, p.192.

[5] Quoted in J. N. D. Kelly, *Golden Mouth: The Story of John Chrysostom*, London, Duckworth, 1995, p.137.

[6] Walter Hilton, *The Scale of Perfection*, New York, Paulist Press, 1991, pp. 234f.

[7] The full poem can be found in *The New Oxford Book of Christian Verse*, edited by Donald Davie, Oxford, OUP, 1981, p.100; and elsewhere.

[8] Quoted in O.Clément, *op cit*, p.193.

[9] In *The Syriac Fathers on Prayer and the Spiritual Life*, introduced and translated by Sebastian Brock, Kalamazoo, Cistercian Publications, 1987, p.70.

ALSO PUBLISHED BY SLG PRESS

Prayer: Meditative Texts
Gilbert Shaw

The Power of the Name: The Jesus Prayer in Orthodox Spirituality
Kallistos Ware

The Simplicity of Prayer (texts)
Mother Mary Clare

Prayer and Meditation for a Sleepless Night (leaflet)

Praying the Word of God
Charles Dumont

The Hidden Way of Love
Barry Conaway

Mixed Life
Walter Hilton (translated by Rosemary Dorward

A Great Joy: Reflections on the Meaning of Christmas
Kenneth Mason

Bede and the Psalter
Benedicta Ward

A complete List of Fairacres Publications, comprising over
seventy titles, is available on request